T0199056

Giving Thanks

Shaila Karkera
Illustrated by: Elenei Rae Pulido

Copyright © 2017 by Shaila Karkera. 752815
Library of Congress Control Number: 2017900885

ISBN: Softcover   978-1-5245-7737-7
       Hardcover   978-1-5245-7738-4
       EBook   978-1-5245-7740-7

All rights reserved. No part of this book may
be reproduced or transmitted in any form or by
any means, electronic or mechanical, including
photocopying, recording, or by any information
storage and retrieval system, without permission in
writing from the copyright owner.

Print information available on the last page

Rev. date: 01/20/2017

To order additional copies of this book,
contact:
Xlibris
1-888-795-4274
www.Xlibris.com
Orders@Xlibris.com

Giving Thanks

Shaila Karkera
Illustrated by: Elenei Rae Pulido

Thanks for the bright
morning light.

Thanks for rest and shelter
of the dark night.

Thanks for the stars in
the purple night sky.

Thanks for white
clouds billowing by.

Thanks for the shade
of green trees.

Thanks for red flowers and
yellow humming bees.

Thanks for all creatures
big and small.

Thanks for my toys,
especially my ball.

Thanks for teachers and
friends who care.

Thanks for all the
laughs we share.

Thanks for my family, so sweet.

Thanks for nutritious
food to eat.

Thanks for the hugs
and kisses I get.

Thanks for the rains that
get me all soaking wet.

Thanks for all the love
in me to give.

Thanks for a safe place to live.

Thanks for the green
grass where I can play.

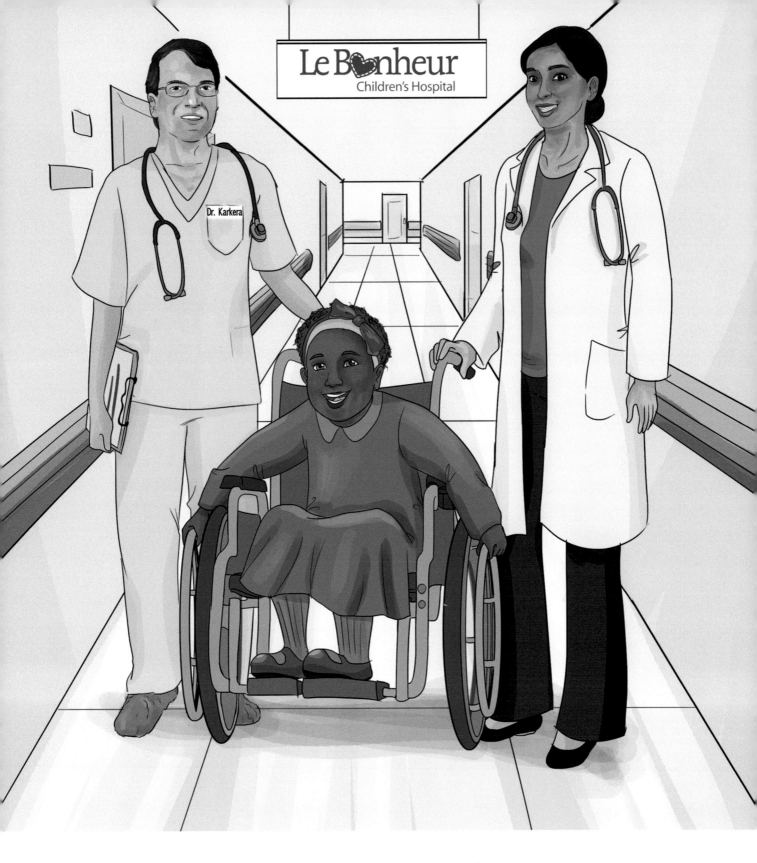

I am grateful every single day.

Thanks for blue birds that sing.

Thank you, God, for just
about everything!

Printed in the United States
By Bookmasters